BOOK 2
Revised

THEORY PAPERS

Robert Pace

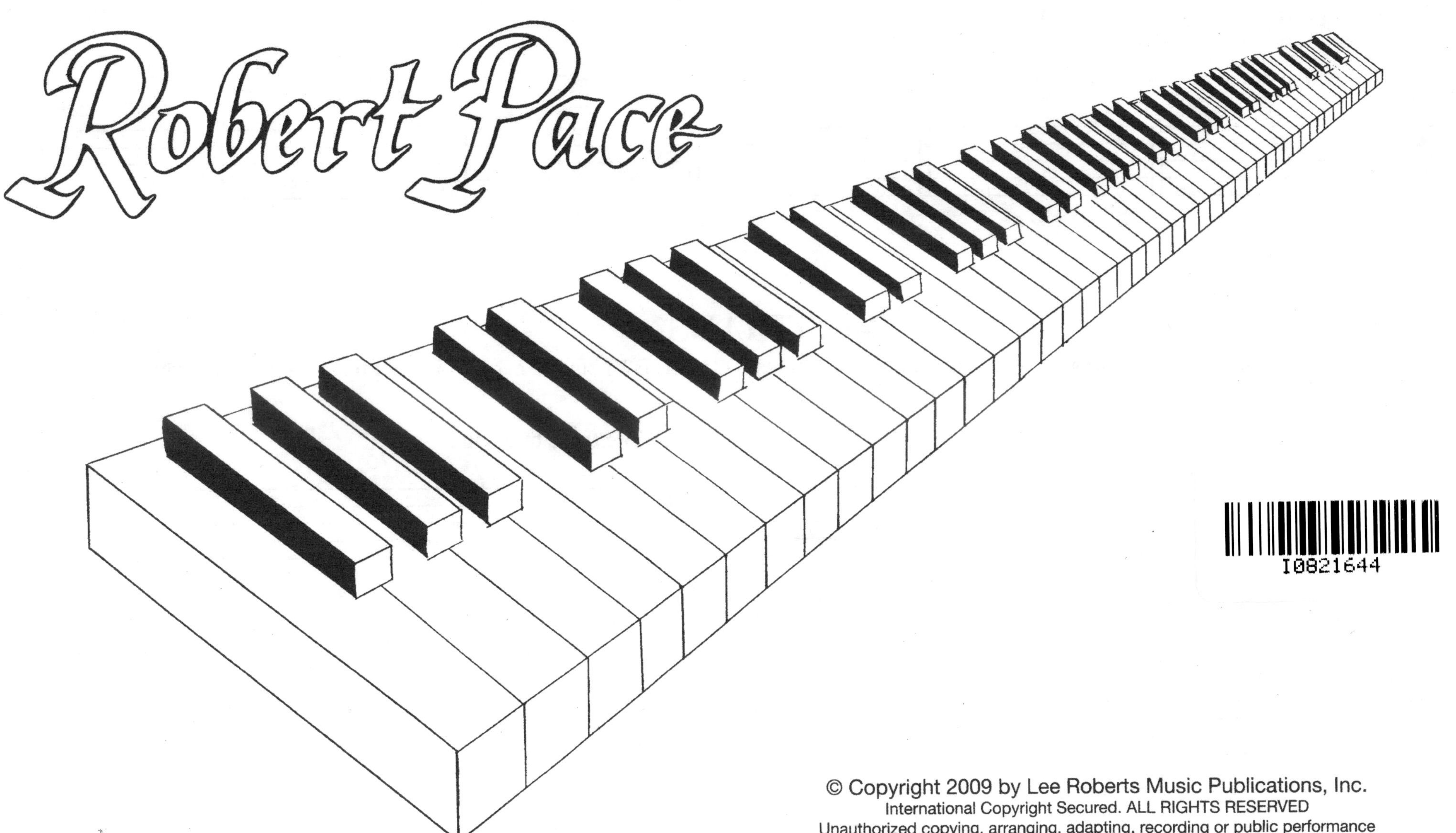

I0821644

KEY SIGNATURES

1. The first day write each of these major sharp key signatures.

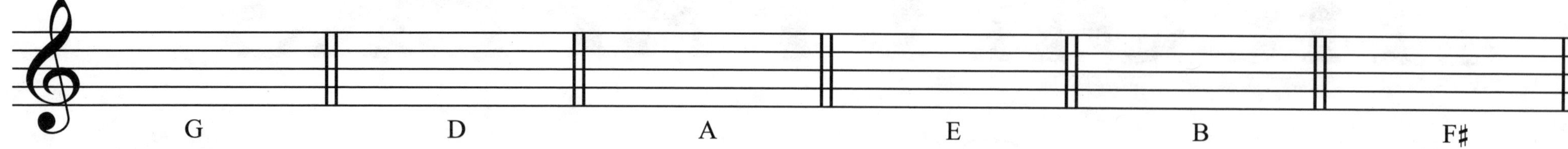

2. The second day write each of these major flat key signatures.

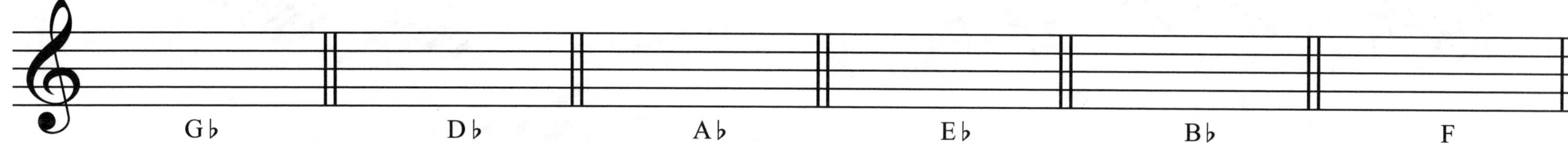

TRIADS

Notice that in both flats and sharps you used the same letter names (G D A E B F) but in sharps you went from 1 sharp to 6 while in flats you went from 6 flats to 1.

3. Write the following major triads in treble clef.

Write these triads in bass clef.

4. Now lower the third (middle tone) of each triad to make it minor.

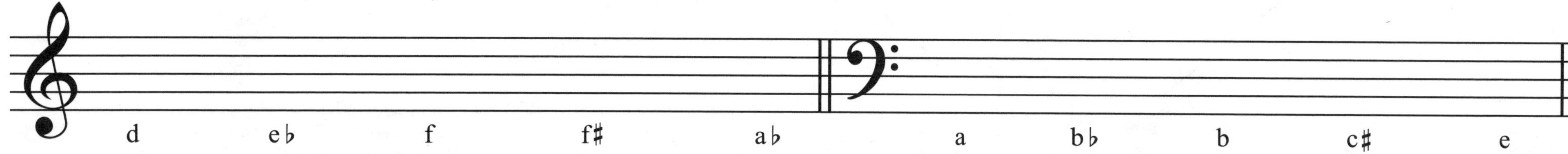

REVIEW

1. To name any sharp key signature, count *up* one line or space from the last sharp. Count *down* one line or space for minor. Fill in the names of these major and minor key signatures.

2. To name *major flat* key signatures, look at **the next to last flat** (F major with only one flat is the exception). To name *minor flat* key signatures, count *down* a 3rd from the **next to last flat**. (Again, one flat, d minor, is the exception).

3. Write the key signature and I V7 I chord progression for these keys.

E♭ Major

F Major

A Major

KEY SIGNATURE

1. Each day practice naming the major and minor key signatures with the Key Signature Flash Cards. After a few days, write these key signatures.

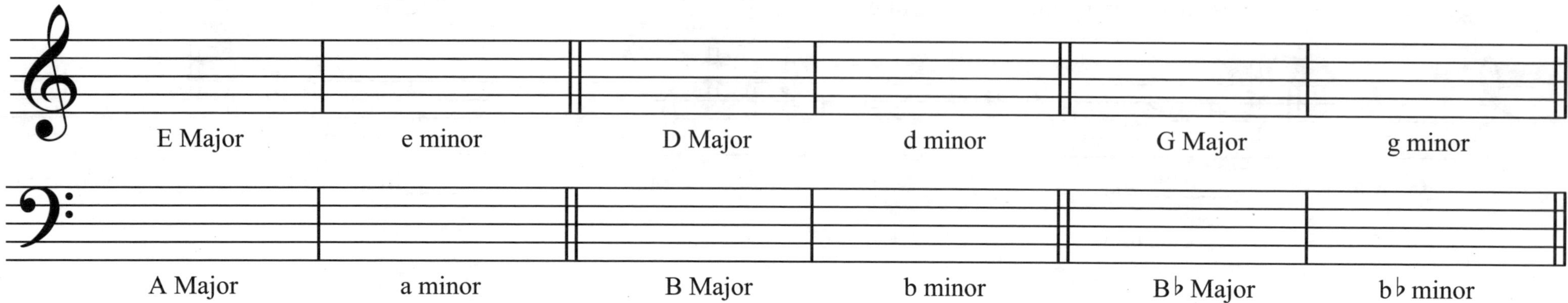

TRIADS

2. Practice naming the major and minor triads with the Major and Minor Flash Cards. Fill in the following triads.

CHORD PROGRESSION

3. Write the I V7 I chord progression in these keys:

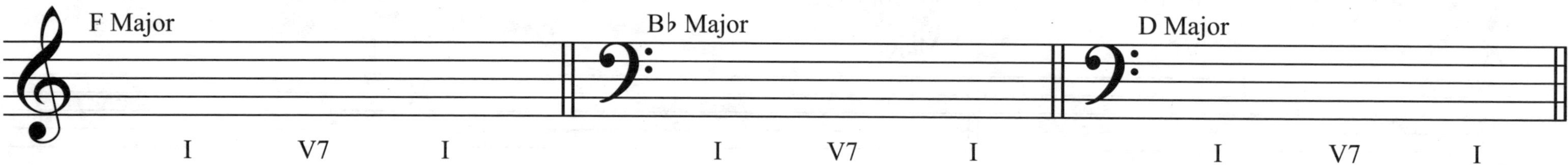

CHORD TONES

1. The tones of this melody are found in the chords of the left hand. They are called *chord tones* (CT).

PASSING TONES

2. A tone between two chord tones is called a *passing tone*. Play this example then circle the *passing tones*.

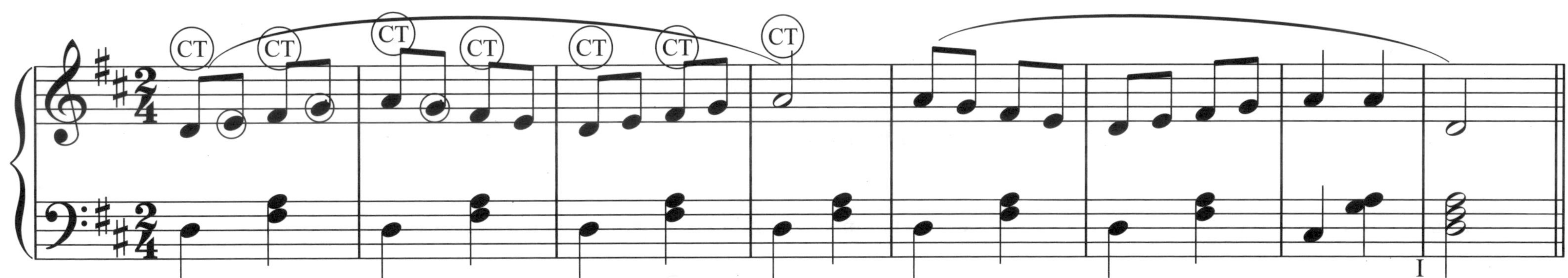

3. First mark the chord tones (CT) in this melody, then play and transpose to E and G major.

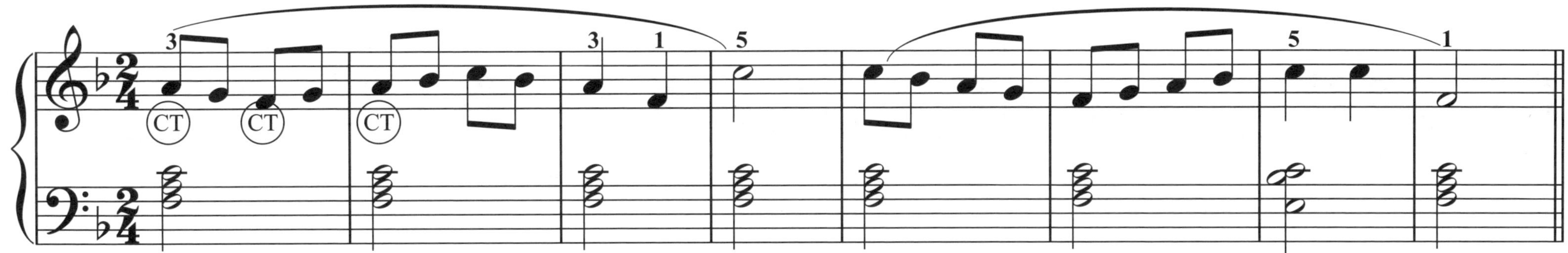

INTERVALS

1. An *interval* is the distance between two tones of music. Here are the intervals between two tones of a C major scale. Notice that the 2nd, 3rd, 6th, and 7th are called *major intervals*. The 4th, 5th, and octave are called *perfect intervals*. Play these intervals each day and try to name them without looking at your book.

Write the upper note of each interval, then play them and try to identify each by its sound.

CHORD TONES AND PASSING TONES

2. Mark all of the chord tones (CT) and passing tones (PT) in this melody. Play as written then transpose to other keys.

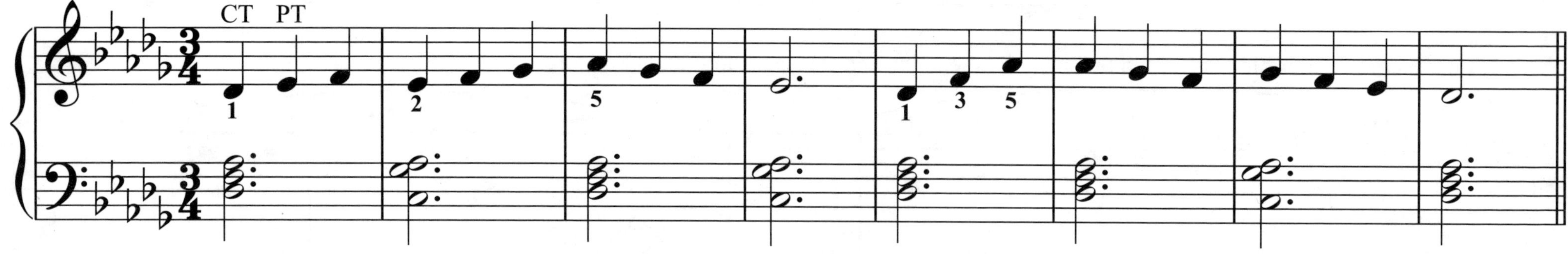

INTERVALS

1. Write the upper note for each interval and add the necessary flats or sharps. Do not use the key signature for these intervals. For major use " + " and for perfect intervals use " P ".

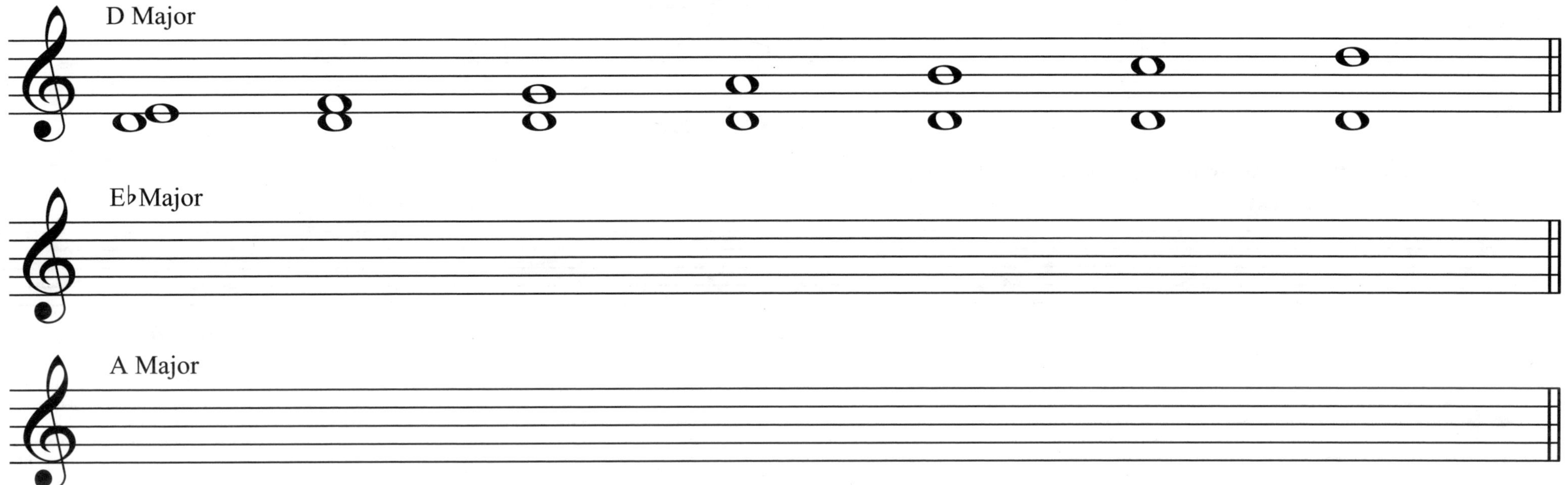

DORIAN MODE

2. Write a melody in the Dorian Mode, using any white keys from D to D, and harmonize it with "open fifths" in the bass.

MAJOR KEY SIGNATURES

1. Write the following major key signatures.

INTERVALS

2. Complete the following intervals with the proper accidentals for G and G♭ Major.

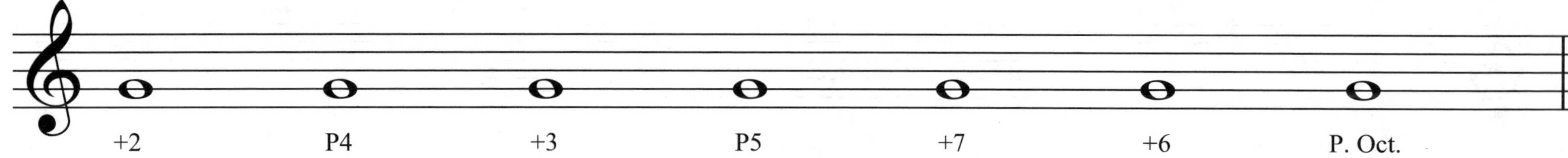

MAJOR AND MINOR TRIADS

3. Practice with both the Major and the Minor Flash Cards, then fill in each triad. Play each set daily.

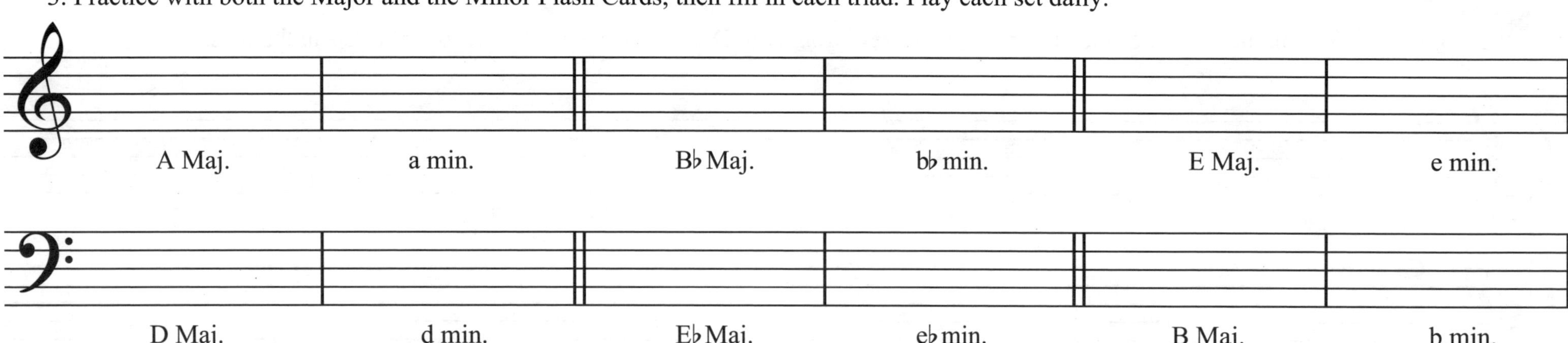

MELODY HARMONIZATION

1. Major and minor triads can move up or down the major scale to harmonize a melody. Fill in the missing triads then play the melody.

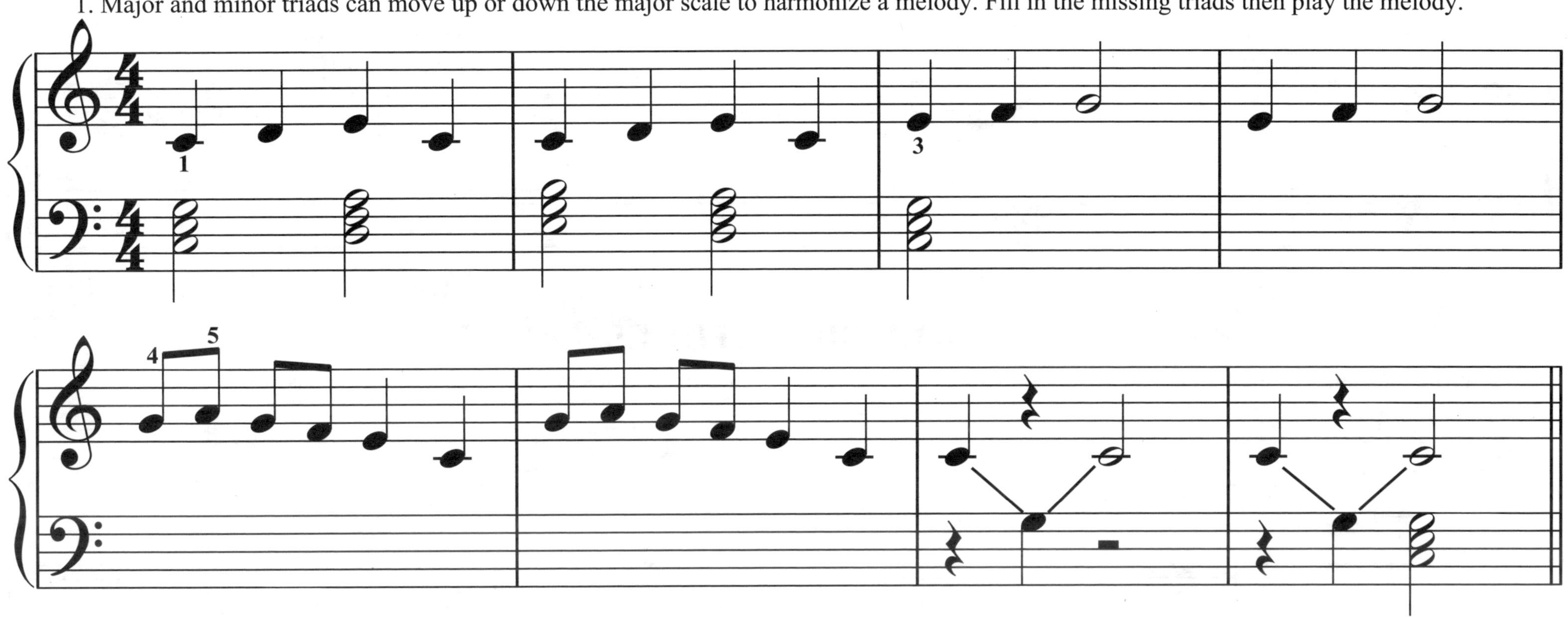

CREATING AND HARMONIZING A MELODY

2. Complete this melody and harmonize it with I and V7 chords.

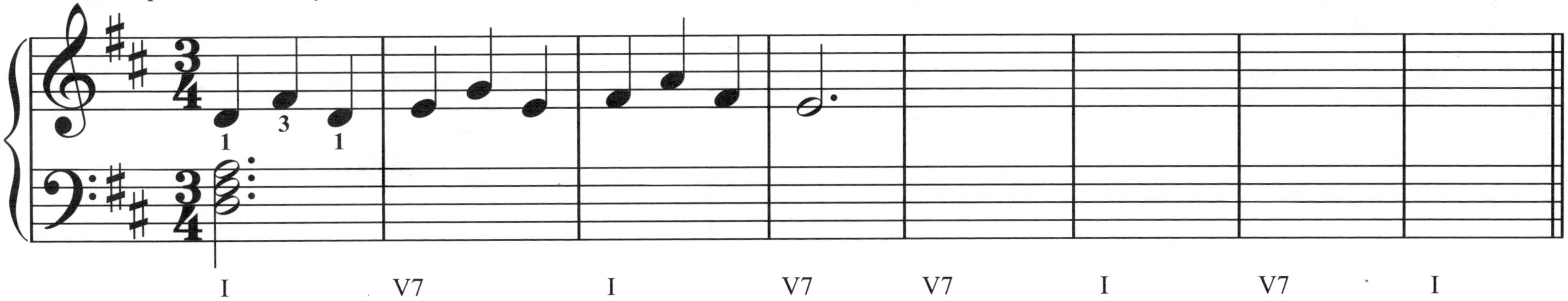

1 3 1

I V7 I V7 V7 I V7 I

NEIGHBOR AND PASSING TONES

1. Complete the chords in the bass part, then label the passing tones (PT), the upper neighbors (UN), and the lower neighbors (LN) in the melody.

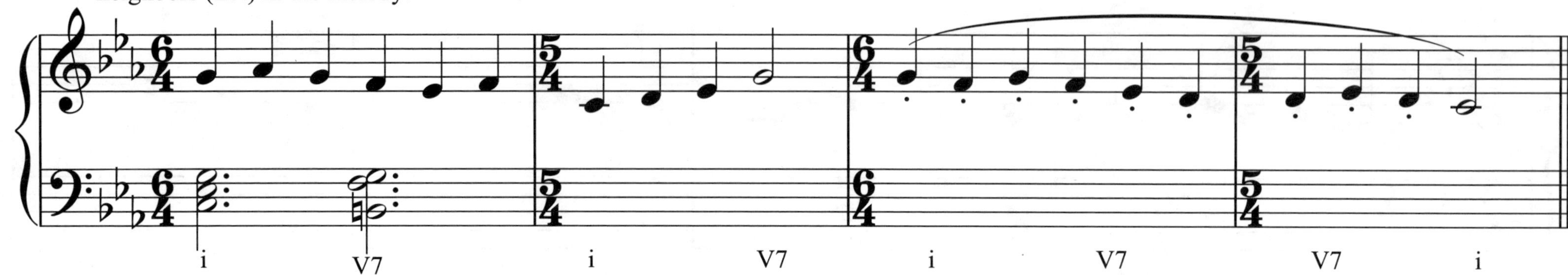

KEY SIGNATURES

2. Write the names of these major sharp key signatures in the treble clef, then make that same key signature in the base clef.

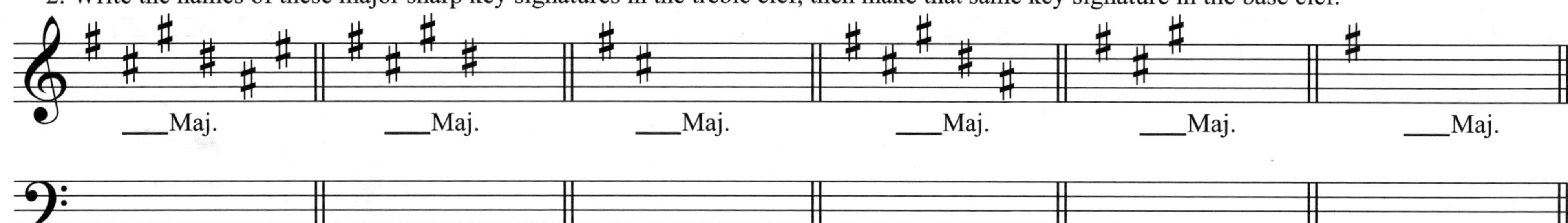

MELODIES WTH PASSING TONES

3. Circle and label any passing or neighbor tones, then play and transpose to D♭ and E♭ major. Also, fill in the missing chords in the bass.

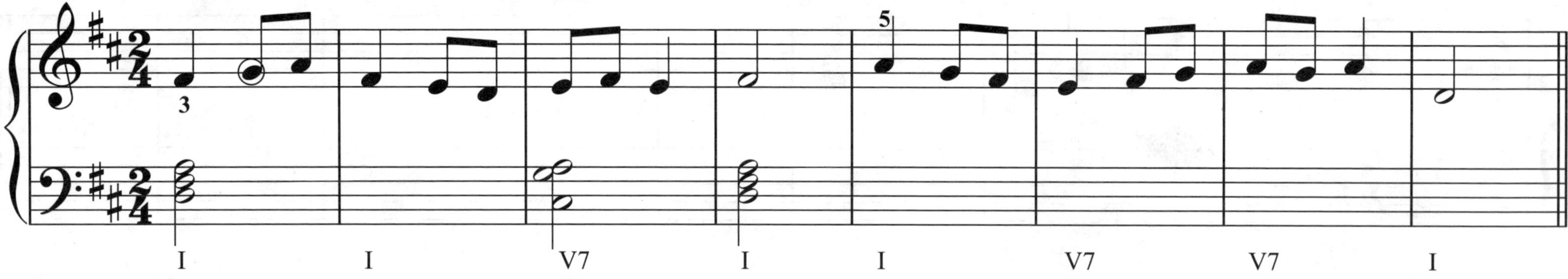

MAJOR AND MINOR TRIADS

1. Write then play these major and minor triads.

CREATING A MELODY

2. Fill in the chords in the bass, then create a melody and play it.

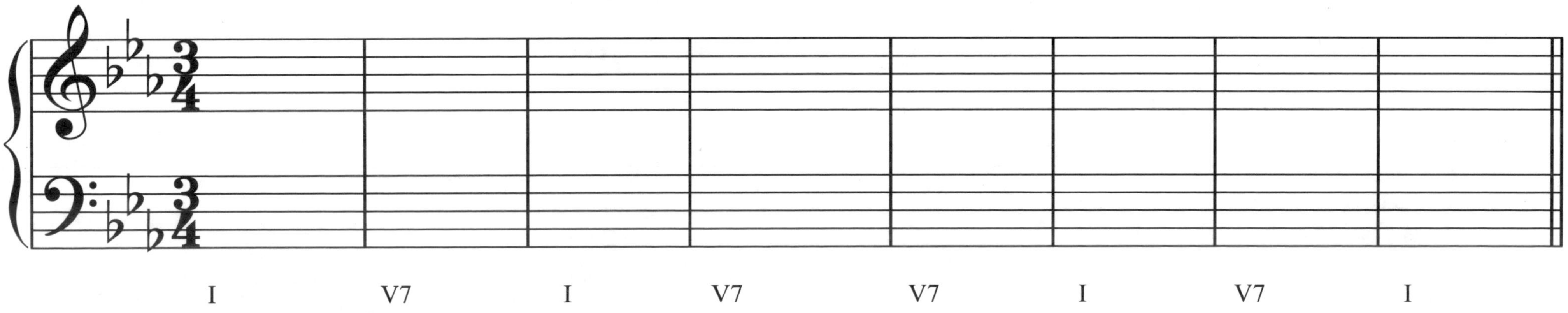

MINOR KEY SIGNATURES

3. Write these minor key signatures in both treble and bass clef.

c minor | b minor | g minor | f minor | f♯minor

TONE ROW

1. Play this new *row* several times to get its sound and say the number as you play it.

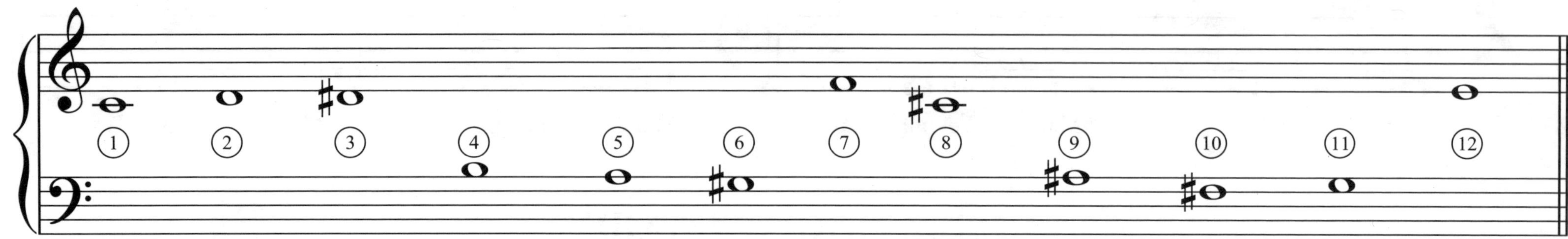

TWELVE TONE MELODIES

2. After playing as written several times, change the rhythm to create other melodies.

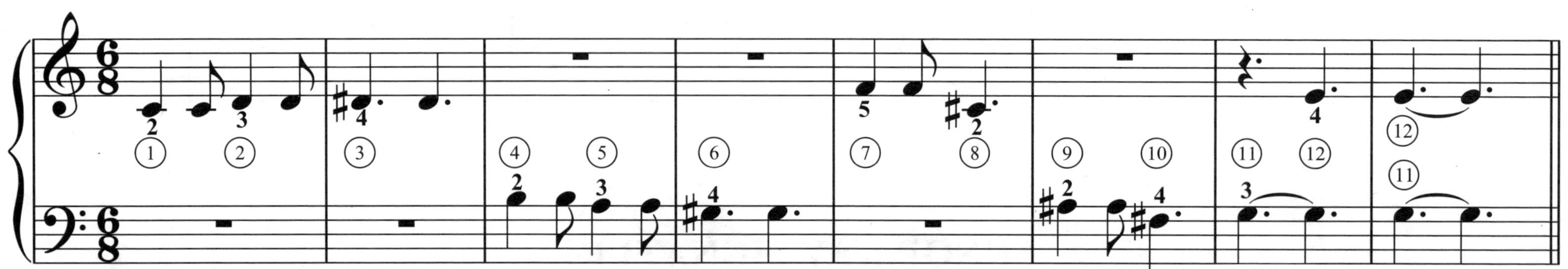

REVIEW

3. Write, then play the I V7 I chords in these keys:

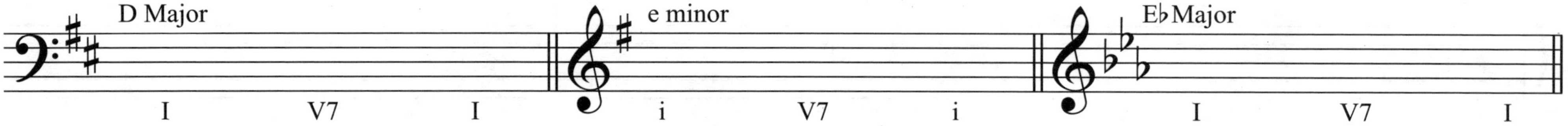

TONE ROW

1. The twelve tones have been rearranged to create a new row. Play it several times to get its sound.

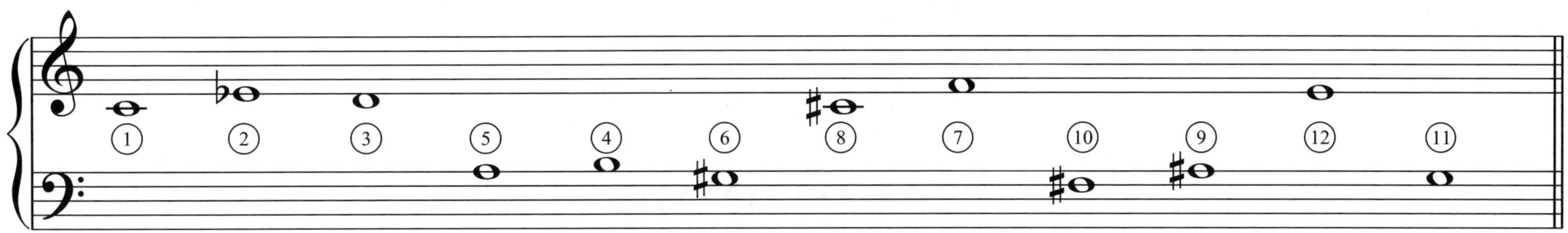

NEW TWELVE TONE MELODY

2. Use the new tone row to create a new twelve tone melody.

KEY SIGNATURE REVIEW

3. Write the following major and minor key signatures.

G♭Major f♯minor c minor B Major f minor A Major

I IV I CHORD PROGRESSION

1. Write the correct key signature, then fill in the I IV I chords.

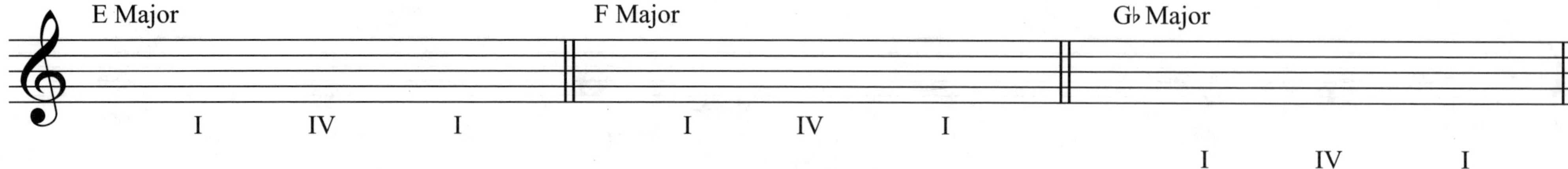

CREATIVE ANSWERS

2. Fill in the chords in the bass, then each day create two new Answers for the Question.

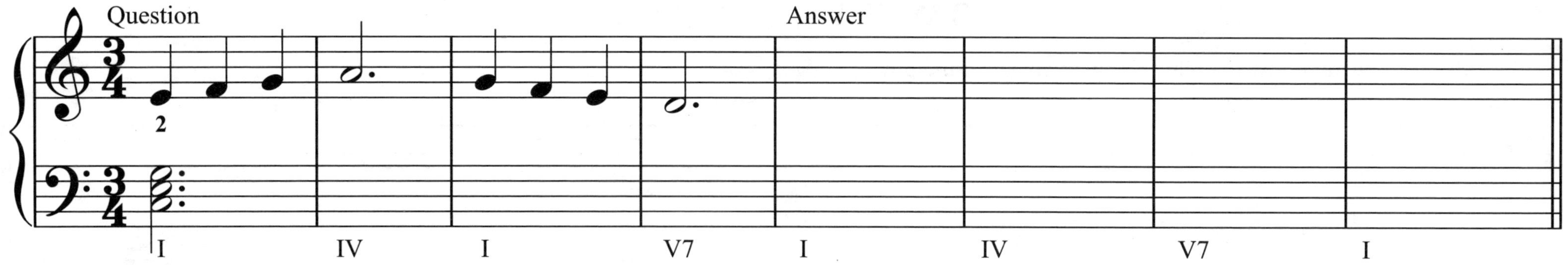

QUESTIONS AND ANSWERS

3. Create and notate a Question and Answer harmonized with I IV and V7 chords.

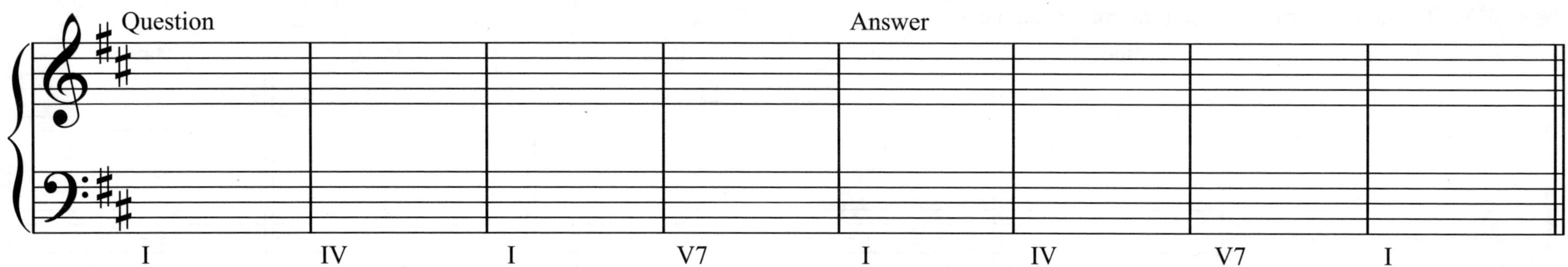

IV CHORD REVIEW

1. Write the key signature, then the I IV I chord progression for each key.

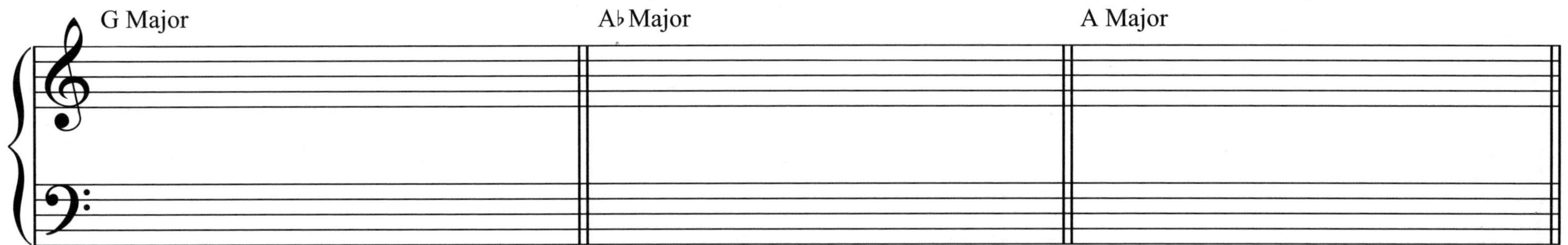

MELODY HARMONIZATION

2. Harmonize this melody with I, IV and V7 chords, then play it. Also create new melodies using the same rhythm and chords.

I IV I CHORDS

1. Make a key signature for B♭, B and D Major, then fill in the I IV I chords for each key.

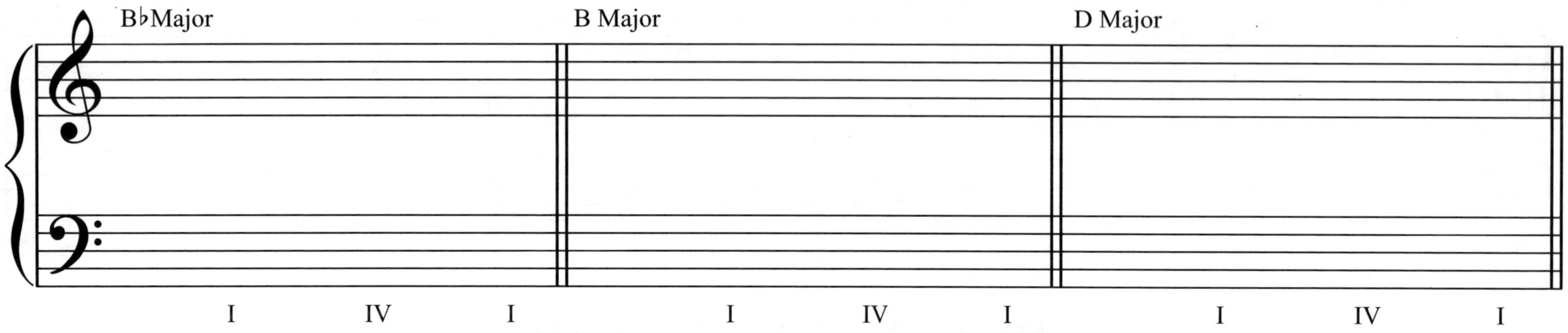

TRIADS AND INTERVALS

2. Write these Major and minor triads, and play each to get its sounds.

3. Write the names of these intervals and play them.

I IV I V7 I CHORD PROGRESSION

1. Here is the I IV I V7 I chord progression in C major. Write this progression in D♭, D and E♭ major, then play all of them each day.

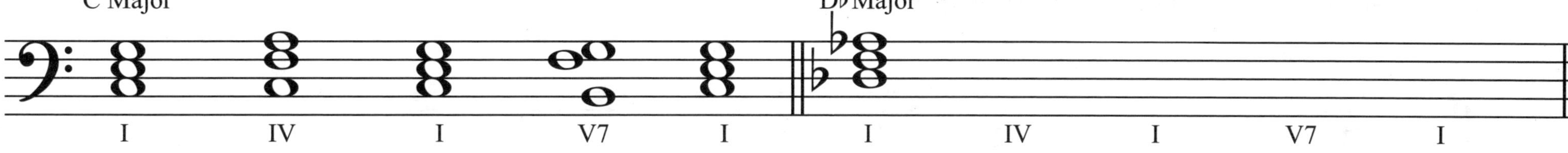

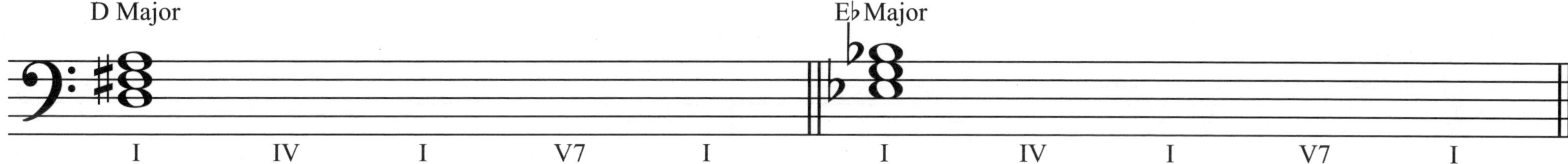

TRIAD AND INTERVAL REVIEW

2. Fill in the upper notes and correct flats or sharps for these major and minor triads, then play and name each.

3. Label these intervals and play each.

I IV I V7 I CHORDS

1. Write, then play these I IV I V7 I chord progressions.

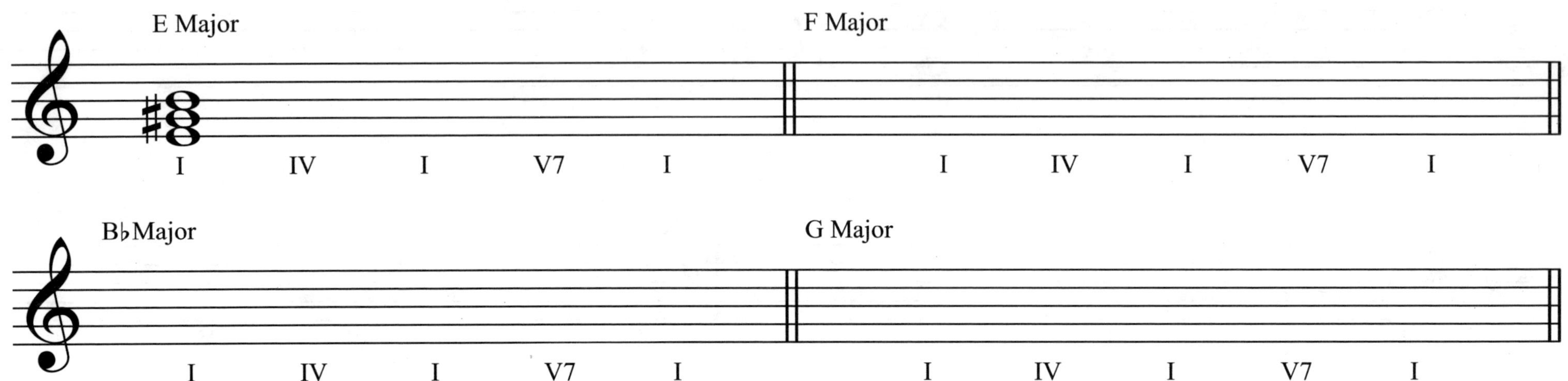

MINOR MELODY

2. First play this minor melody and harmonize it with block chords in the left hand. Next, write the chord numbers under the bass and fill in the notes.

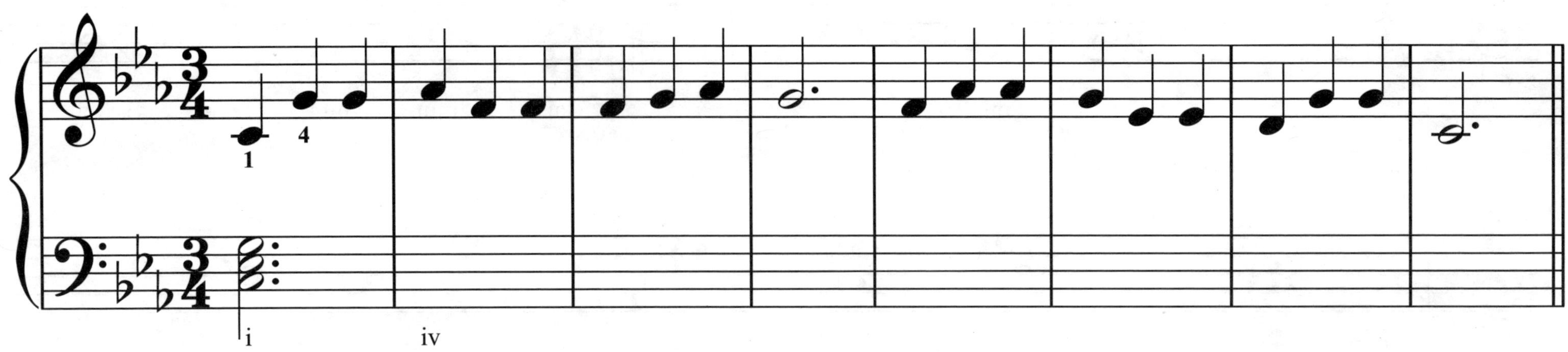

I IV I V7 I CHORDS

1. Write, then play these I IV I V7 I chord progressions. Also review the progressions on page 18.

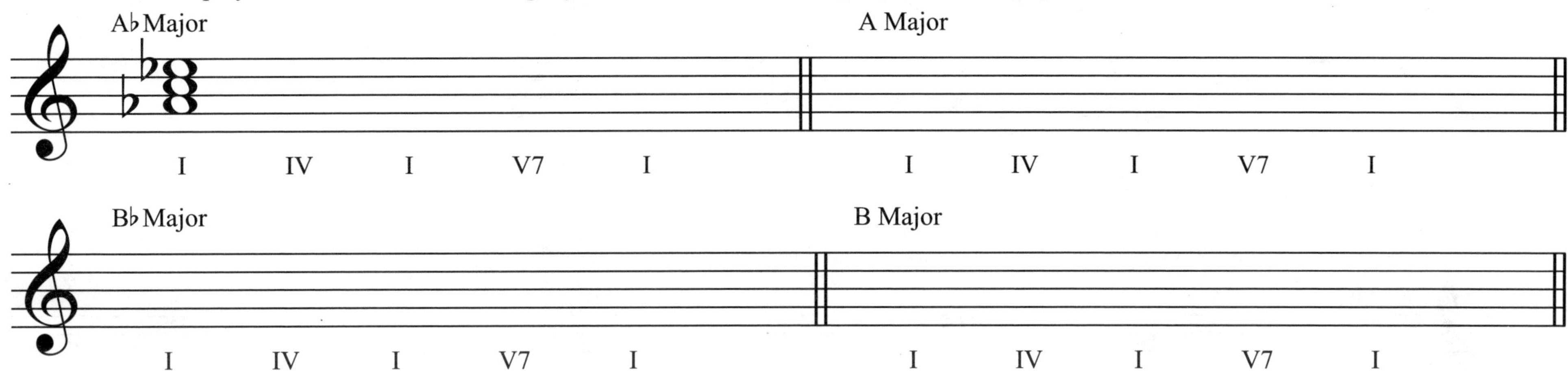

DIMINISHED TRIADS

2. Fill in each minor (—) and diminished (○) triad as shown here and play each to listen to its sound. Also, use your major, minor and diminished flash cards to gain skill in identifying each one.

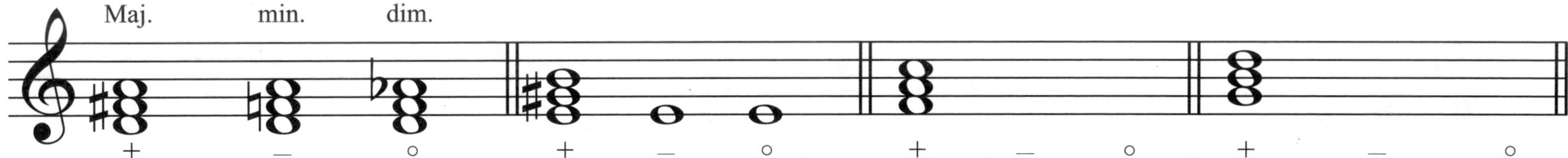

TRIAD REVIEW

3. In the key of F major write a triad on each tone of the scale. Notice that the I, IV, and V are major, while the ii, iii, and vi are minor. The seventh (vii○) is diminished. Be sure to play each triad.

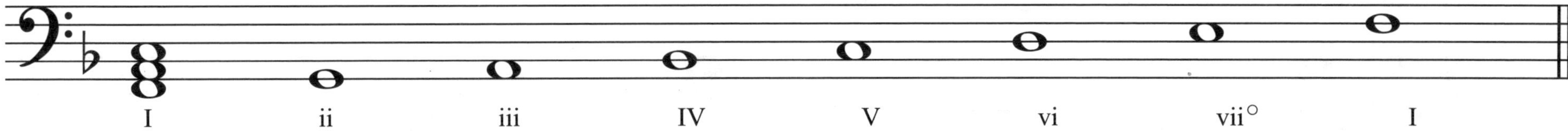

TRIAD AND INTERVAL REVIEW

1. Make a triad of each degree of the A major scale then write the correct number and type of triad.

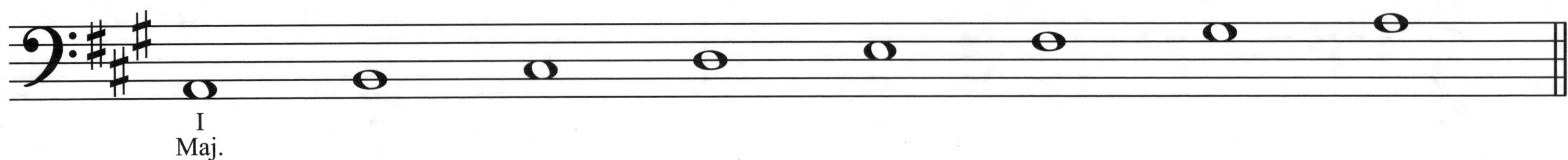

2. Write and play the following major, minor, and diminished triads. Use double flats if necessary.

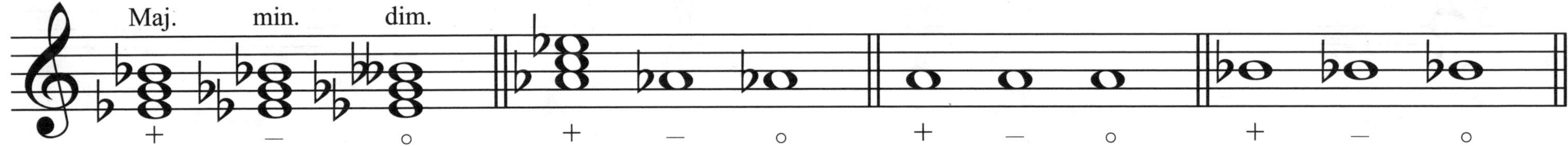

3. Identify and label these intervals.

MINOR CHORD PROGRESSION

4. Write and play the i iv V7 i chord progression in these minor keys.

TRIADS

1. Fill in a triad on each degree of the D Major scale and label each.

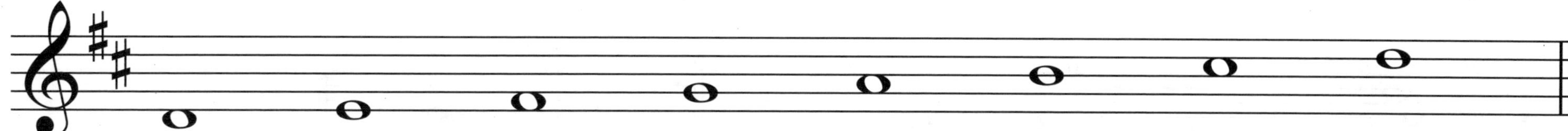

2. Write and play the following Major, minor and diminished triads. There are interesting games you can play with your Major, minor and diminished flash cards. (see your "Musical Games and Activities" book.)

KEY SIGNATURES

3. Make these key signatures.

E Major | f minor | D♭ Major | c minor | A Major | b minor

I IV I V7 I CHORD PROGRESSION

4. Write and play I IV I V7 I chord progressions in these keys.

TRIADS

1. Fill in these major (+), minor (–), and diminishrd (○) triads, then play them to get their sounds.

TRIAD PLAY

2. You can get some interesting sounds by using major, minor and diminished triads moving up or down the major scale. Each day, explore new patterns and see how many you can create.

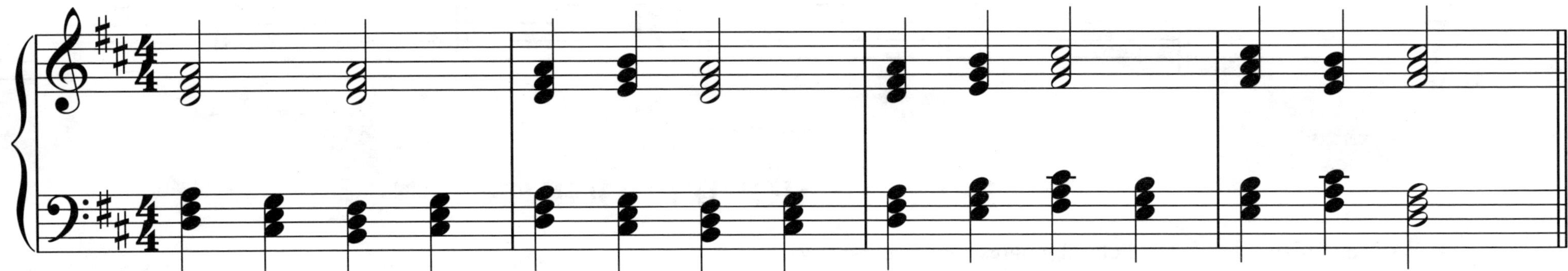

I IV I V7 I CHORD PROGRESSION

1. Write the correct key signature, then fill in the notes for each chord.

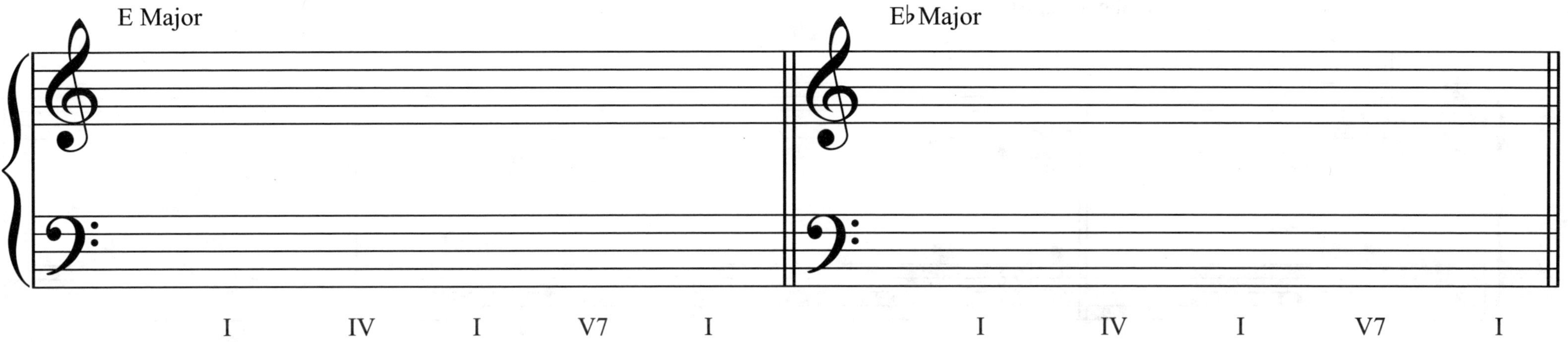

INTERVALS

2. Mark all of the thirds in these melodies with the number "3" and a bracket.

TRIAD REVIEW

1. Fill in the missing notes then play each triad.

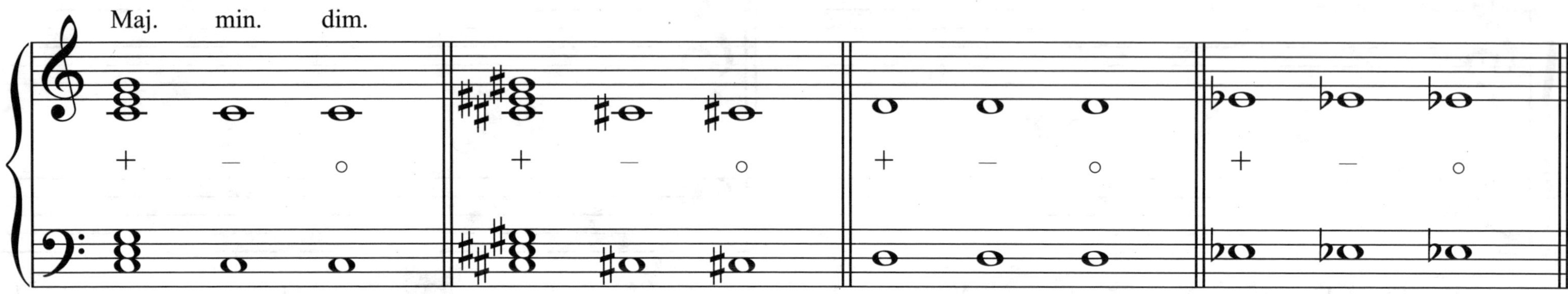

I IV V7 I CHORD PROGRESSION

2. Notice in this I IV V7 I chord progression which tones move and which ones stay. Fill in the missing notes and play each progression.

I IV V7 I CHORDS

1. Fill in the missing chords and play in each key.

E♭ Major | F Major | G Major

I IV V7 I | I IV V7 I | I IV V7 I

INTERVALS

2. If the top note of a major interval is lowered one half step it becomes *minor*. When a perfect interval is lowered one half step it becomes *diminished*.

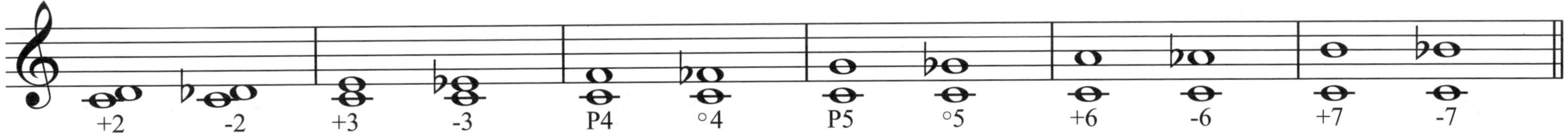

3. Fill in the missing upper notes with the proper accidental.

INTERVAL STUDY

1. Fill in the upper note with the correct accidental for each of these intervals.

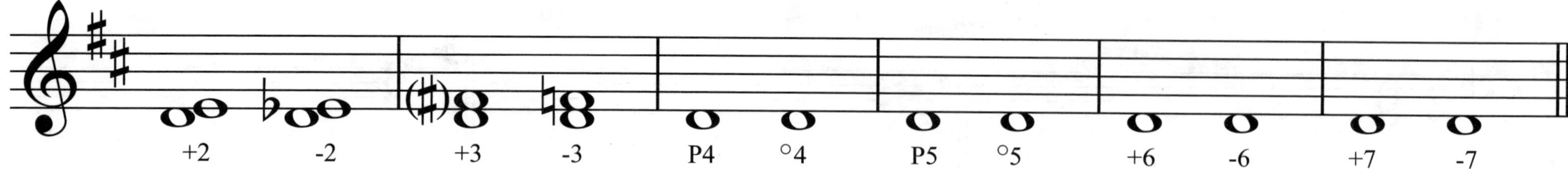

2. Mark each interval in this melody.

REVIEW

3. Write the name of each key signature for both major and minor.

4. Put the bar lines in this melody.

DIATONIC TRIADS

1. Make a triad on each tone of the D Major scale. Write the name of each.

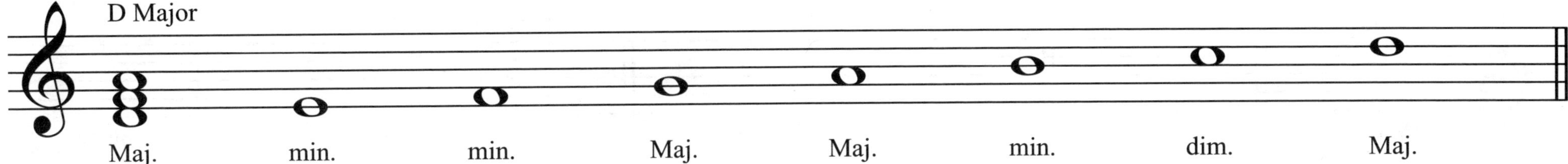

I IV V7 I CHORD PROGRESSION

2. Write the key signature, then the I IV V7 I chord progression.

INTERVALS

3. Write these intervals.

4. Remember that a perfect interval lowered a half step becomes *diminished*. A major interval lowered a half step becomes *minor*. Mark each of these.

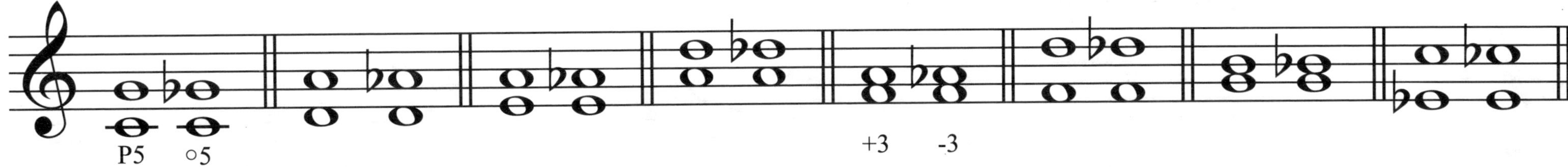

KEY SIGNATURES

1. Write each of these major or minor key signatures.

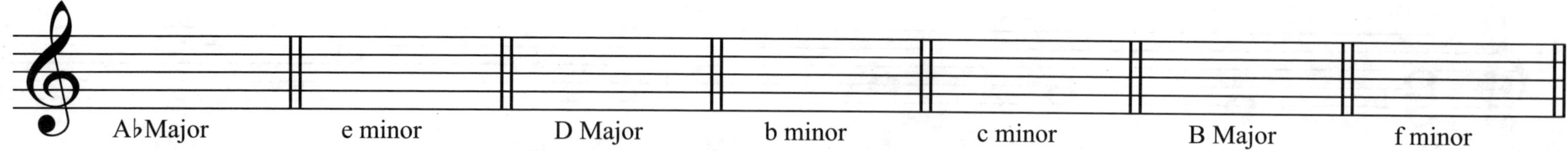

TRIADS

2. Make major, minor and diminished triads on the following notes:

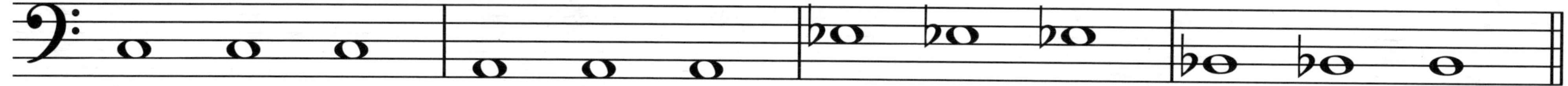

INTERVALS

3. Fill in the top note for these intervals, then play and say the name of each.

I IV V7 I CHORD PROGRESSION

4. Write the I IV V7 I chord progression in these major keys.

MINOR TRIAD GROUPS

1. Here are the four groups of minor triads. Write them as indicated. Also, practice naming them with your Minor Triad flash cards.

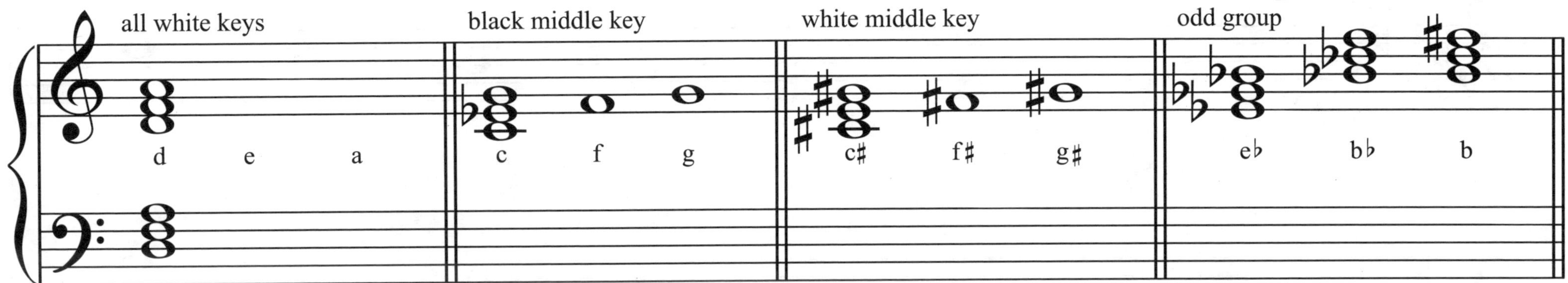

i iv V7 i CHORD PROGRESSION

2. Here is the i iv V7 i chord progression in minor. Fill in the missing notes in the treble clef and play each, then play the progression. Transpose to e♭, e, f and g minor.

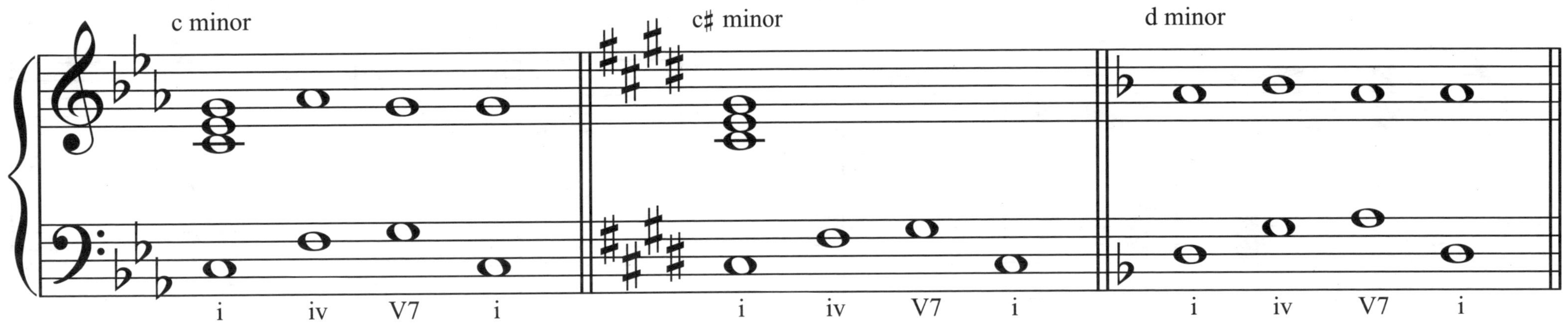

DIATONIC TRIADS

1. Make a triad on each tone of the D♭ and A♭ Major scales and write the name of each.

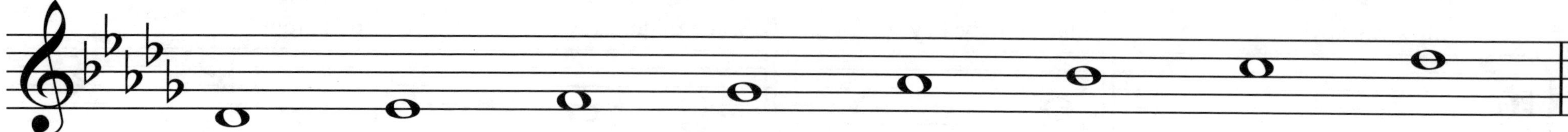

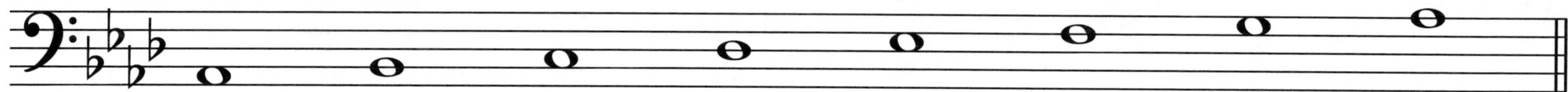

HARMONIZING A MELODY

2. Complete this melody and harmonize it with triads moving up or down the scale by steps.

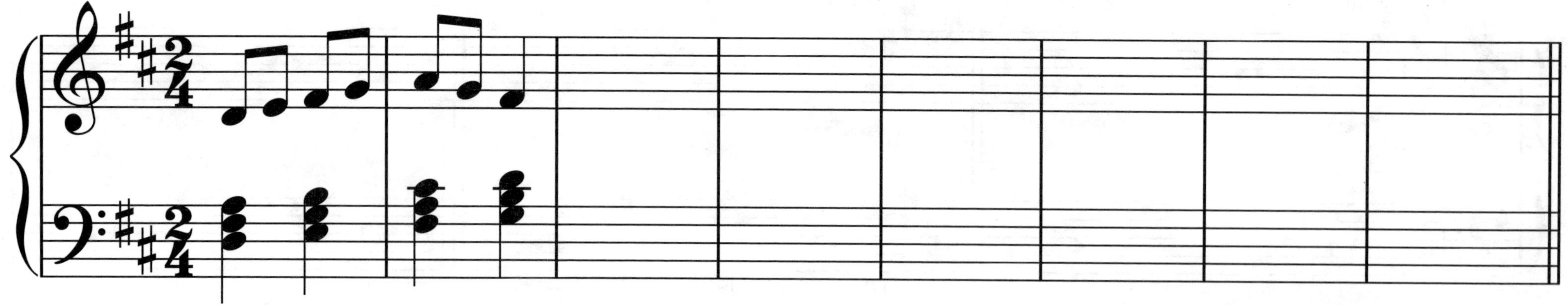

WALTZ BASS

1. Harmonize this melody with the I IV V7 chords using a waltz bass.

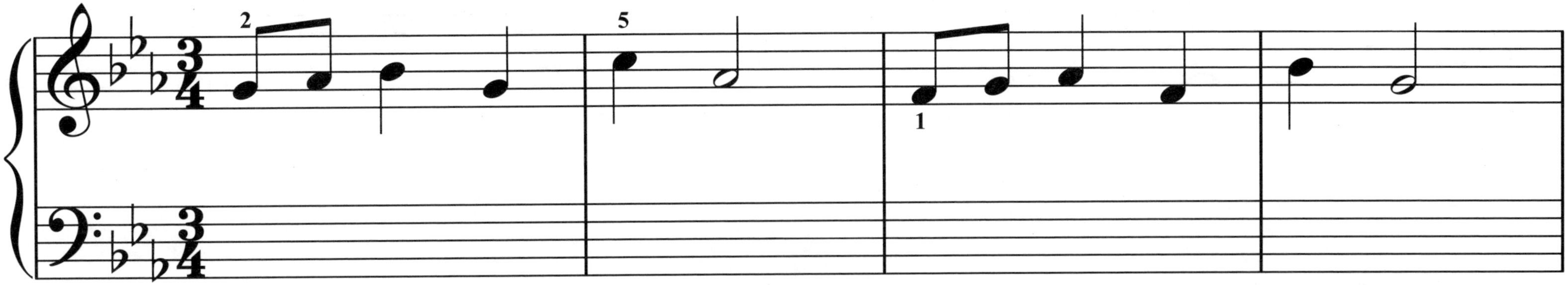

TRIAD REVIEW

2. Write, then play these triads.

INTERVALS

1. Write these intervals in the key of E♭ Major.

TRIADS

2. Write these triads and play each to get its sound.

MELODY HARMONIZATION

3. Harmonize this melody, then play it in the keys of E and E♭ Major.

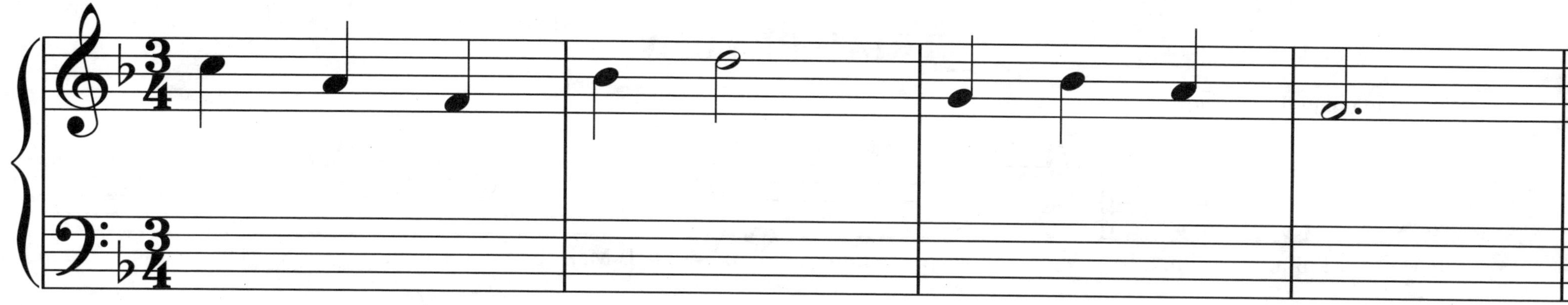

KEY SIGNATURES

1. Write these key signatures.

A Major | D♭Major | c minor | f♯ minor | B♭ Major | b♭ minor | b minor | F♯ Major

TRIAD REVIEW

2. Write these major, minor and diminished triads then play them each day. Also, practice with your Major, Minor and Diminished Triad Flash Cards.

D+ d– d○ | E♭+ e♭– e♭○ | G+ g– g○ | B+ b– b○ | F+ f– f○

NEIGHBOR AND PASSING TONES

1. Mark the neighbor tones (UN and LN) and passing tones (PT) in this melody. Also write the correct chords in the bass.

I IV V7 I CHORD PROGRESSION

2. Write the key signature and the I IV V7 I chord progression for each of these keys.

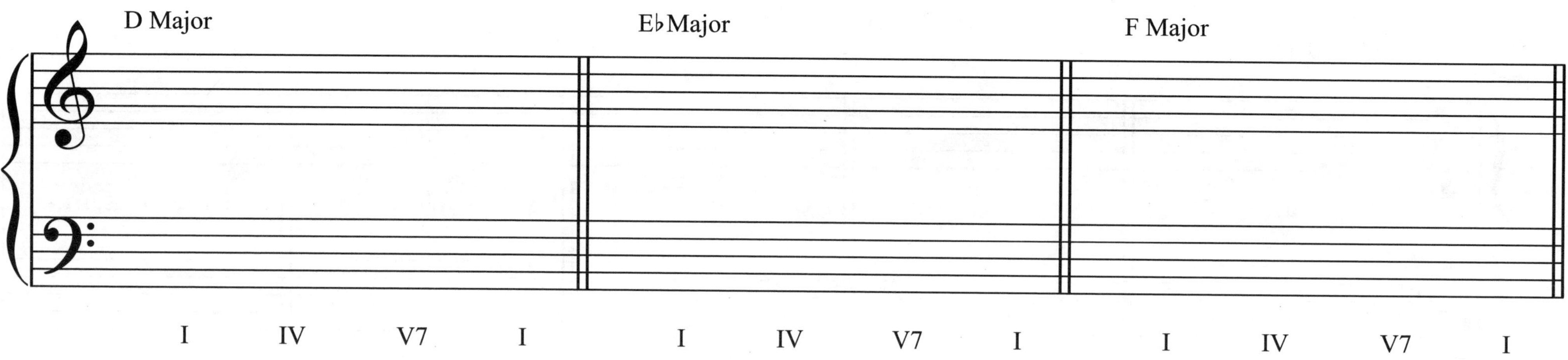

TRIAD REVIEW

1. Write the following major, minor and diminished triads, then play all of them each day. Also, practice with your Triad Flash Cards.

F Maj. f min. f dim. | E Maj. e min. e dim. | G Maj. g min. g dim. | C Maj. c min. c dim.

i iv V7 i CHORD PROGRESSION

2. Write the minor key signature and the i iv V7 i chord progression for each of these keys.

c minor | d minor | e minor

i iv V7 i | i iv V7 i | i iv V7 i

INTERVALS

1. Write and play these intervals.

TRIADS

2. Make a triad on each degree of the scale and write its name.

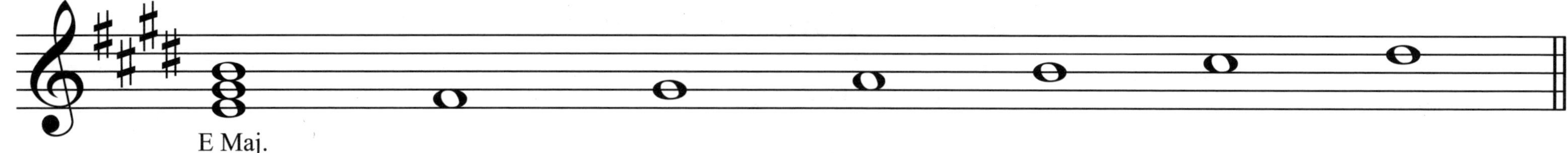

MAJOR AND MINOR TRIADS

3. Write these major and minor triads and play them each day. Use your Triad Flash Cards to gain speed in recognizing these.

MINOR KEY SIGNATURE REVEIW

1. Write these minor key signatures.

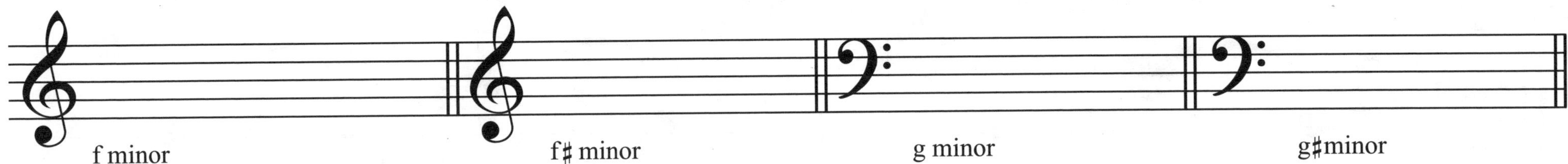

BI-CHORDAL SOUNDS

2. Complete this bi-chordal example by writing either major or minor triads for both treble and bass parts. Identify each chord.

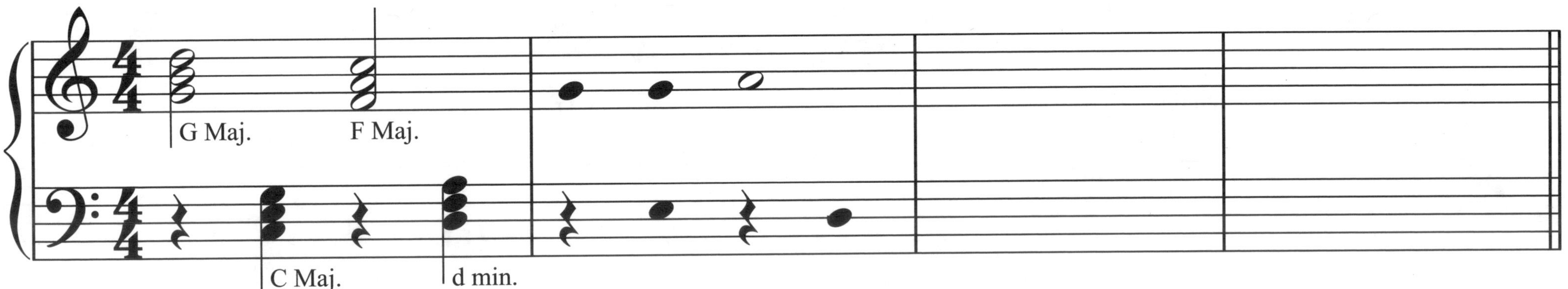

SAILOR BOY

3. Complete the melody and the harmony for this example. Also play it in several other keys such as G♭, F and E Major.

INTERVALS

1. Write the number name of each interval and play each to get its sound.

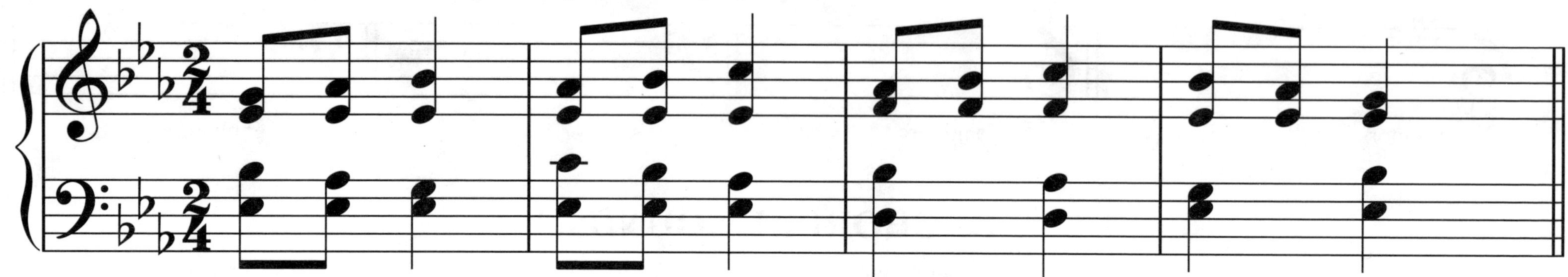

TRIAD REVIEW

2. Write a major, minor and diminished triad for each of these tones and drill with your Triad Flash Cards.

CHORD PROGRESSION

3. Fill in the correct notes for this chord progression then play each one.

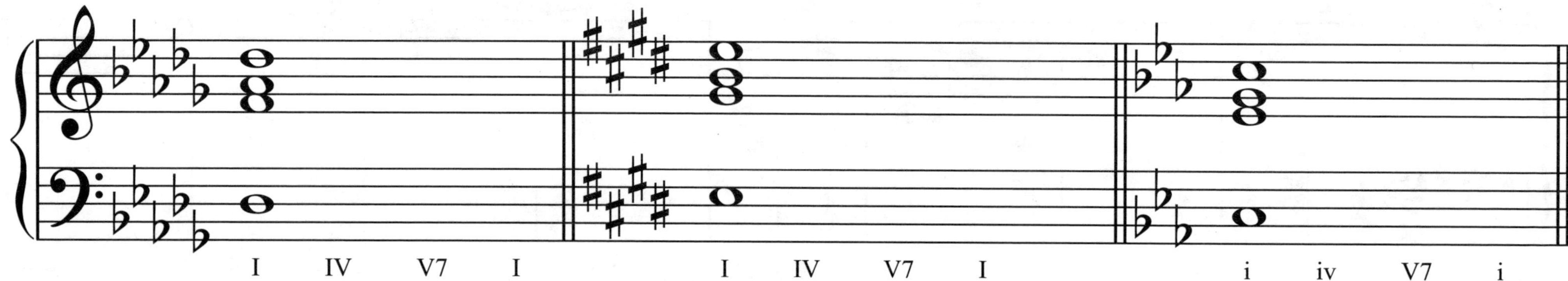

QUESTION AND ANSWER

1. Create and notate an Answer to this Question with the two parts moving in either parallel or contrary motion.

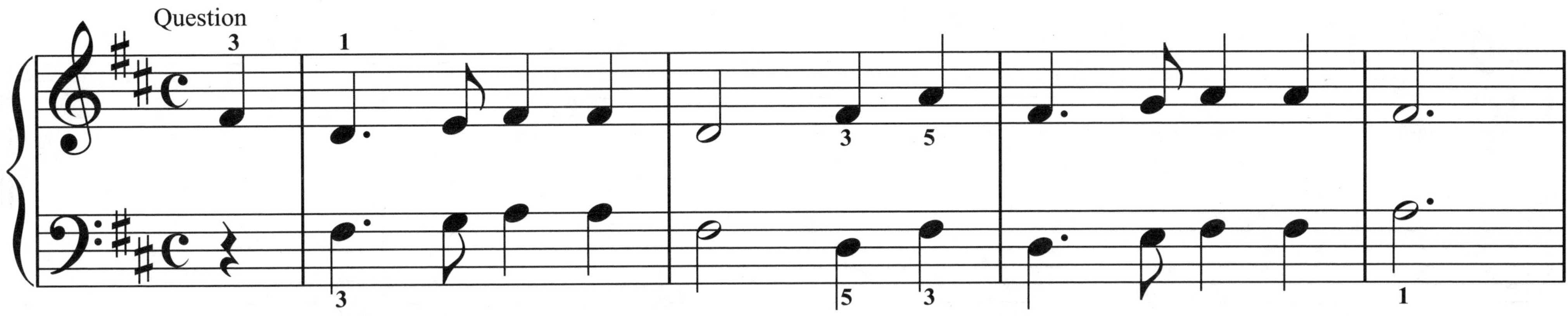

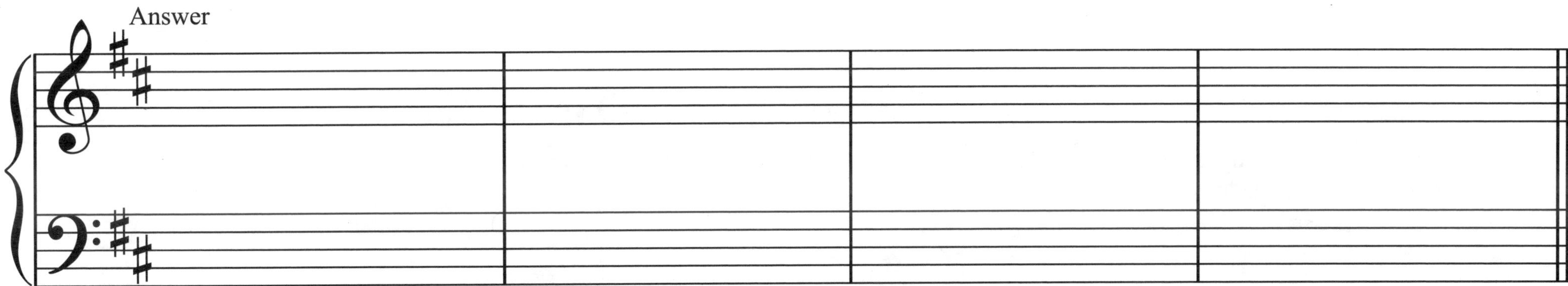

2. Harmonize this melody with the i iv V7 i chords, then create other melodies to harmonize with the same chord progression.

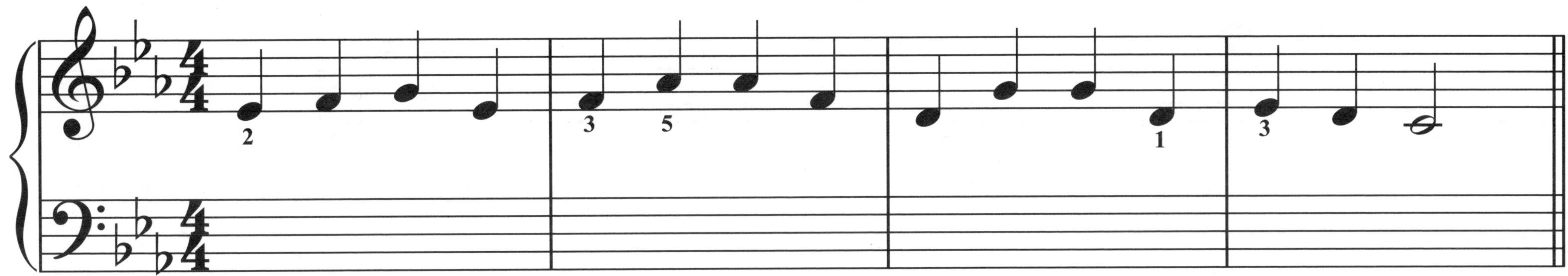

CHORD PROGRESSION

1. Write and play these chord progressions.

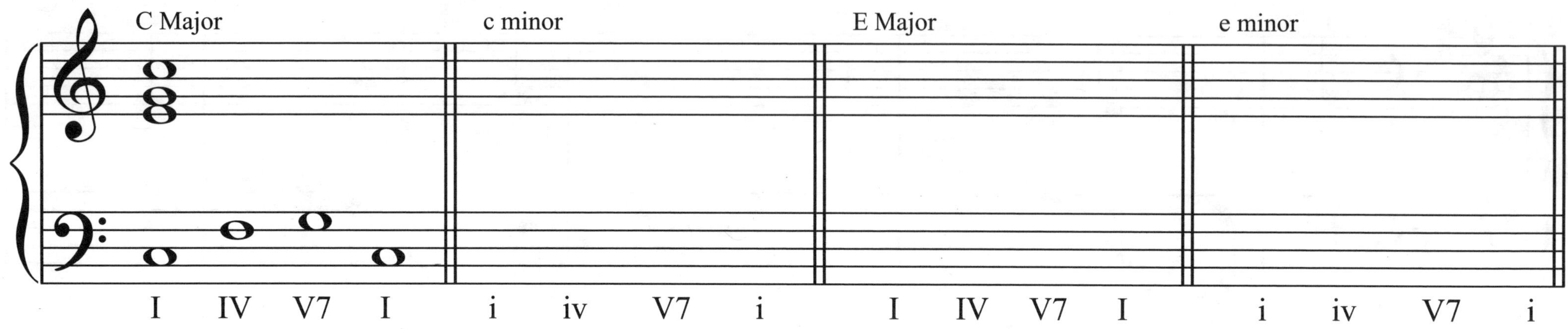

HARMONIZING A MELODY

2. Harmonize this melody and write the number of each chord. Also mark the chord tones (CT), passing tones (PT), and neighbor tones (UN or LN) in the melody.

TRIAD REVIEW

1. Write and play these triads.

INTERVALS

2. Write and play these intervals.

CREATING A MELODY

3. Complete the melody and accompaniment for this chord pattern.

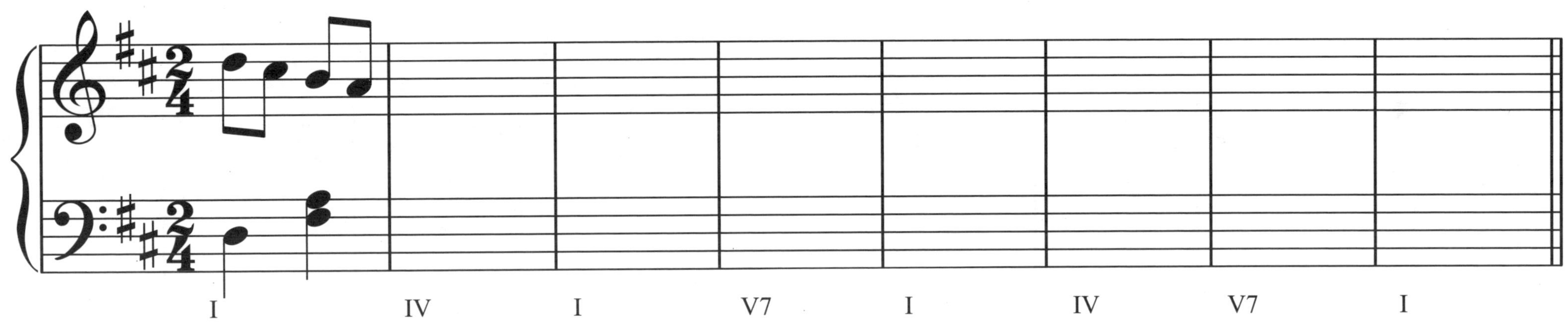

INTERVALS

1. Write the name of each interval below the bottom note and play each.

TRIADS

2. Write these triads then play them.

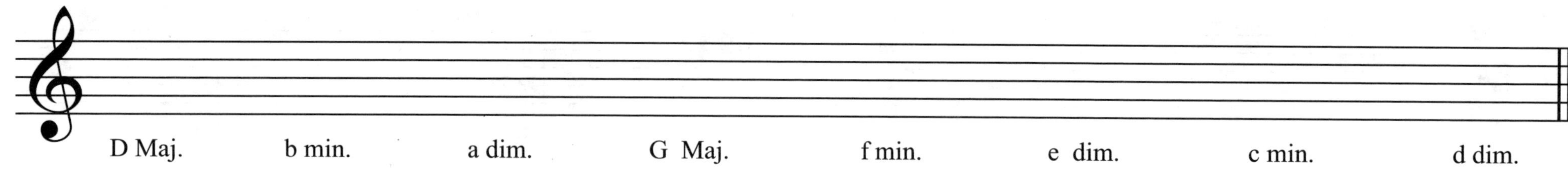

DIATONIC TRIADS

3. Harmonize this melody with major, minor or diminished triads moving up or down the scale.

INTERVALS

1. Fill in the upper note for each of these intervals.

TRIADS

2. Fill in the correct upper notes and accidentals for these triads.

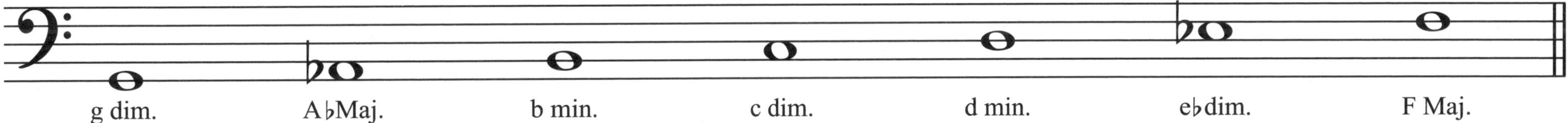

MELODIC TONES

3. Harmonize this melody, then mark the passing tones (PT), lower neighbors (LN) and upper neighbors (UN). Also mark the sequences.

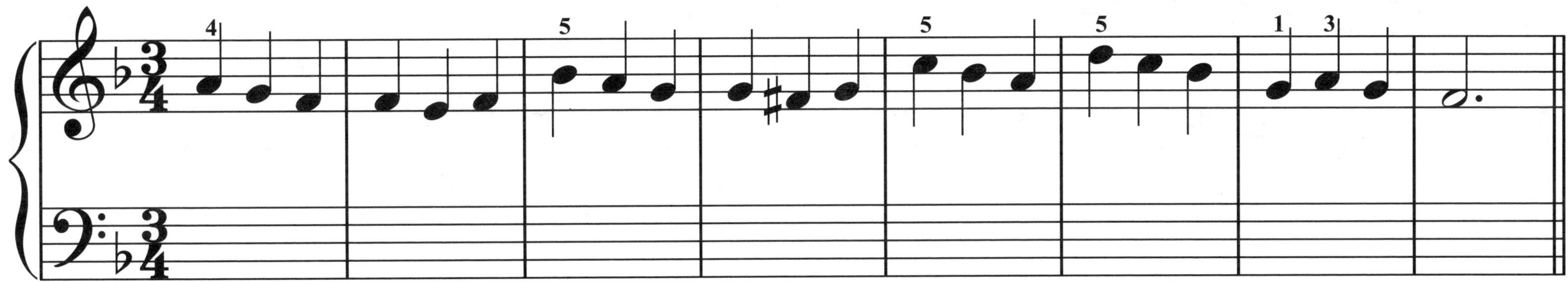

I IV V7 I CHORD PROGRESSION

1. Write and play the I IV V7 I chord progression in these keys, then transpose up and down by half steps to other keys.

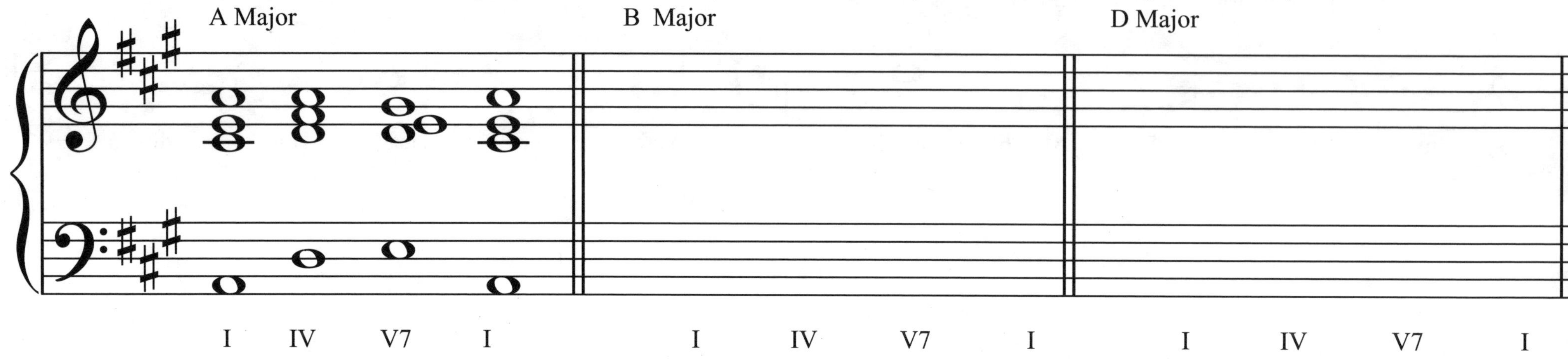

CREATING AND HARMONIZING A MELODY

2. Complete this melody and harmonize it with a waltz bass. Transpose to C, E, and F Major.

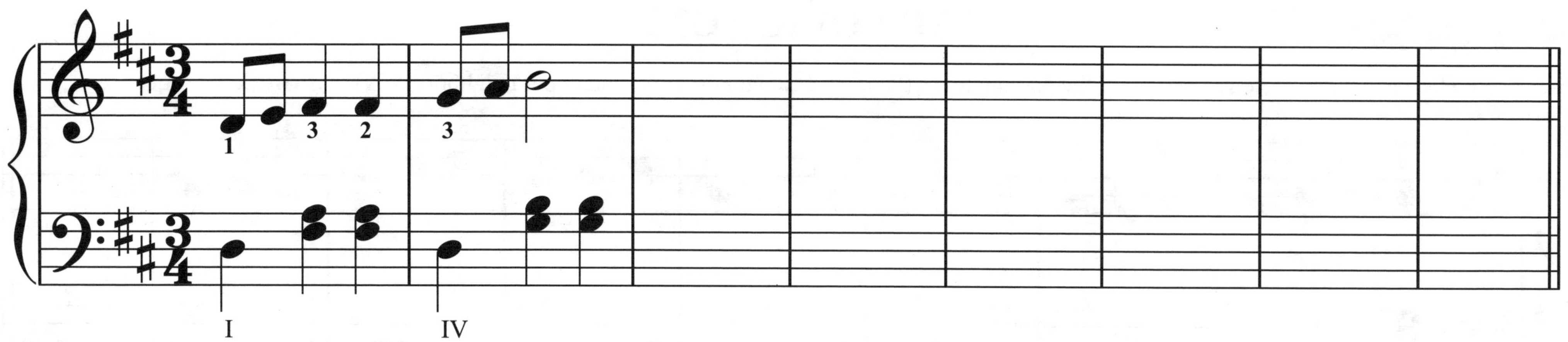

MINOR CHORD PROGRESSIONS

1. Write and play the i iv V7 i chord progression in these keys:

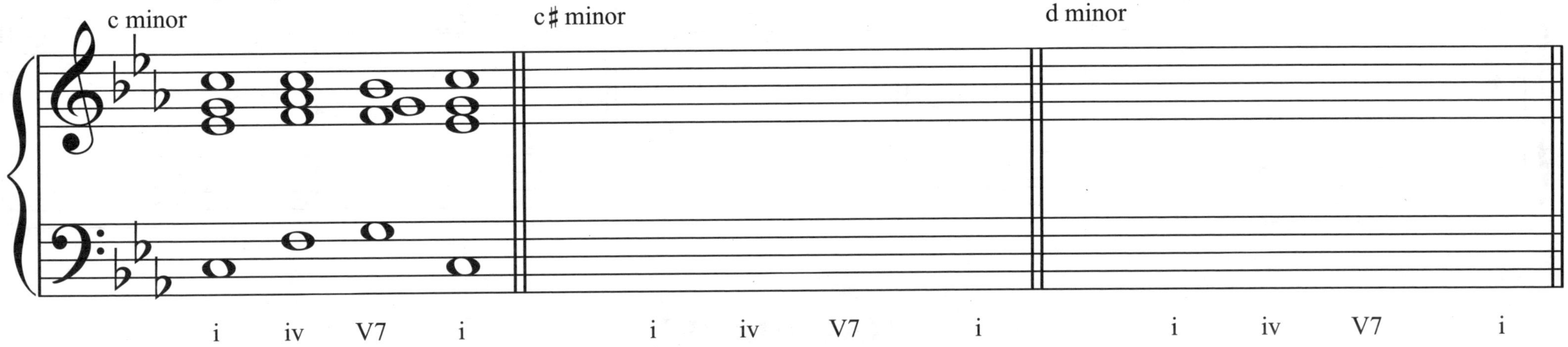

HARMONIZING A MELODY

2. Harmonize this minor melody, then mark the passing tones (PT) and upper neighbors (UN).

KEY SIGNATURES

1. Write these key signatures in both clefs.

E Major c minor D♭Major f♯minor g minor

TRIAD REVIEW

2. Fill in the correct notes and accidentals for these triads.

I IV V7 I CHORD PROGRESSION

3. Fill in the I IV V7 I chord progrssion in these Major keys:

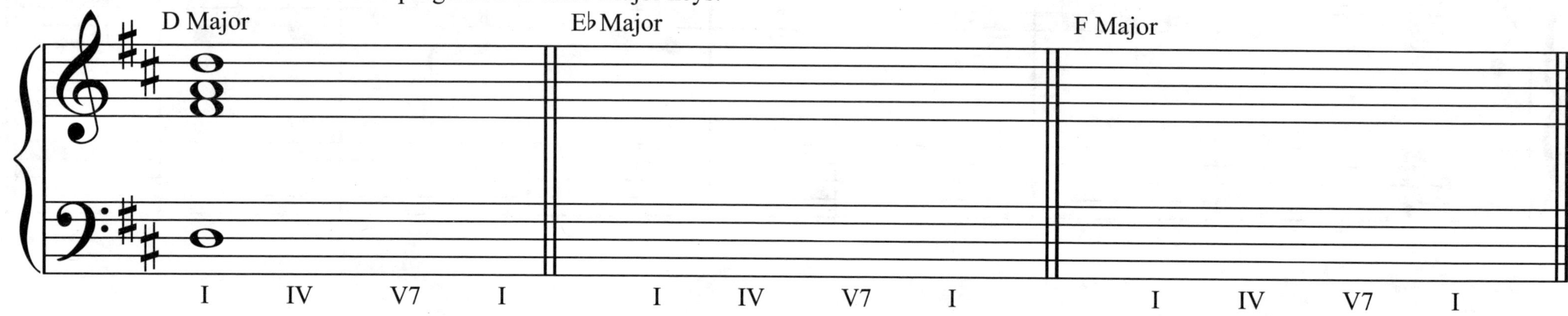

TRIAD REVIEW

1. Fill in the upper note with any necessary accidentals for these intervals and play each.

NEIGHBOR AND PASSING TONES

2. Label all neighbor and passing tones in the melody. Also, fill in the chords in the bass.

i iv V7 i CHORD PROGRESSION

3. Fill in the i iv V7 i chord progression in these minor keys:

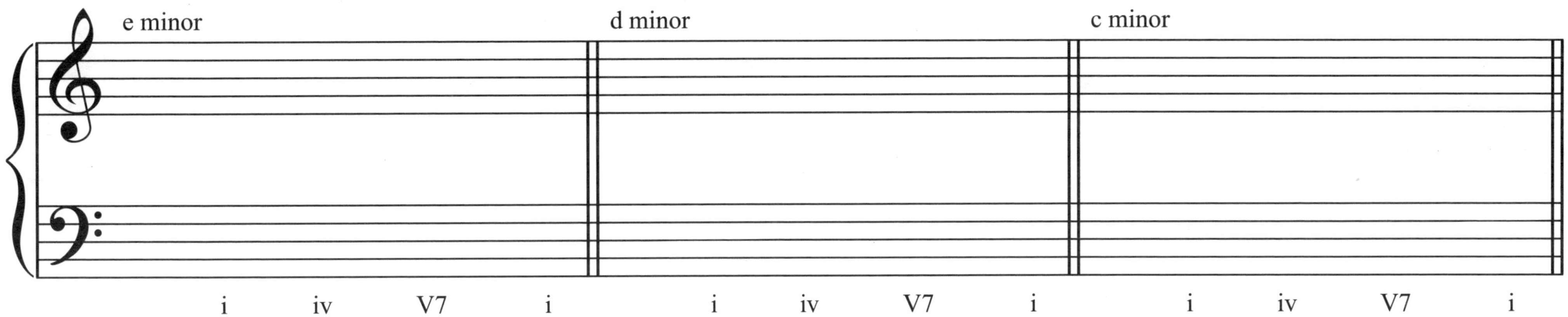